Gifting Empathy

The Selfless Gift that Cultivates

Understanding and Bonding between

Parents and Teens

Other Books by Dr. Buckingham

You Deserve More: A Single Woman's Guide to Marriage

Resilient Thinking: The Power of Embracing Realistic and Optimistic Thoughts about Life, Love and Relationships

Can Black Women Achieve Marital Satisfaction? How Childhood Nurturing Experiences Impact Marital Happiness

Unconditional Love: What Every Woman and Man Desire in a Relationship

A Black Man's Worth: Conqueror and Head of Household

A Black Woman's Worth: My Queen and Backbone

Qualified, Yet Single: Why Good Men Remain Single

www.realhorizonsdlb.com

Gifting Empathy

That Selfless Gift that Cultivates
Understanding and Bonding between
Parents and Teens

Dwayne L. Buckingham, Ph.D., LCSW, BCD

An Imprint of RHCS Publishers

RHCS

Gifting Empathy

Additional copies of this book may be purchased online at www.realhorizonsdlb.com or by contacting:

R.E.A.L. Horizons Consulting Solutions, LLC

8101 Sandy Spring Rd, Suite 250

Laurel, MD 20707

240-280-1008 Voice mail

ISBN: 978-0-9855765-5-4

Edited by Aja Jackson

Cover Design by RHCS Publishing

For Worldwide Distribution

Printed in the United States of America

Dedication

To every parent who gives all that they can to nurture and develop productive and healthy youth.

Message to Parents

You have been provided one of the most rewarding, but challenging, opportunities in the world: helping another human being find meaning in his or her life. In this day and age, many people feel that parenting is a burden because many children are disrespectful and disobedient. As you reflect on your teen years, do you remember a time when you thought about or behaved in opposition of what your parents desired? If you answered no, then this book might not help you much. However, if you answered yes, you are on your way to acquiring peace of mind and establishing a better connection with your teen. As you take this educational journey with me, I pray that you have an open mind and heart so that you can gain understanding and acquire knowledge that will enable you to parent with empathy.

Flip the Script (Poem)

I give my all, but my teen feels that I am too strict

So I ask myself often, will I feel the same if
I Flip the Script

Lost in a haze with no way to predict,

I wonder if my bond with my teen would be stronger if
I Flip the Script

I walk away from my teen when I am presented with a
fit, but maybe I could better understand him or her
better if I Flip the Script

When I was a teen I did not feel understood and my
heart was ripped, but now I can prevent a cycle with my
teen if I Flip the Script

If my teen is lost and feels unequipped, I might be a
source of inspiration if I Flip the Script

When my teen angers me I often flip, but I could be
more compassionate if I Flip the Script

If understanding is gained through empathy,
compassion and not feeling whipped, I guess I can
understand, influence and bond with my teen if I would
just sometimes Flip the Script

Take-Home Message:

It is impossible to connect with anyone, especially your
teen, if you cannot envision what life would be like if
you walked in his or her shoes!

Acknowledgments

To my beloved and deceased mother,

Arlene "Tot" Parent

You gave what you could in order to raise me to be a productive and respectful citizen. I did not make things easy for you during my teen years, but I hope that you are smiling in heaven now. My relationship with you provided the primary inspiration for writing this book.

To my wife

Sandia, you model empathy on a daily basis and set the example for our children to follow. Thank you for being so understanding and compassionate.

To my son and daughter

Dwayne, Jr. and Layla, you gave me that courage to be vulnerable and to love without limits. I pray continued blessings over both of you. Also, I pray that your teen years are filled with happiness.

To the parents I have served over the past 20 years

As a psychotherapist, I am thankful for having the opportunity to have gained additional insight into your experiences with raising teens. Each therapeutic session was very informative and as a result, I have acquired a better understanding of the struggles that millions of parents face daily as they strive to raise their teens to become productive citizens.

Contents

DEDICATION

FLIP THE SCRIPT (POEM)

ACKNOWLEDGMENTS

GIFTING EMPATHY I

PART ONE

UNDERSTANDING TEENS... 1

CHAPTER 1

MUST WE FORGET 2

Parents Just Don't Understand 2
Normal Teen Development - Self-Discovery........................... 4
Must We Forget.. 6
Self-reflection.. 6
Learning from Self-Reflection 12
Benefit of Engaging in Self-Reflection................................. 15
TAKE AWAY POINT.. 17

CHAPTER 2

WITHHOLD THE INSTRUCTIONS 25

Teens Need to Be Heard 25
QUESTIONS FOR REFLECTION AND PROCESSING................. 40

CHAPTER 3

SPEND TIME WITH YOUR TEEN 43

Teens Need Attention 43
Quality versus Quantity Time 48
TAKE AWAY POINT.. 56
QUESTIONS FOR REFLECTION AND PROCESSING................. 56

CHAPTER 4

TROUBLED TEENS 60

How to Identify and Respond To Troubled Teens 60
Troubled Teens 61
Identifying Troubled Teens 62
Troubled Teens Who Seek Trouble............................... 64
Identifying Troubled Teens Who Seek Trouble 65
Responding to Troubled Teens.................................. 66
Solutions for Dealing with Troubled and Trouble-Seeking
Teens: 69

PART TWO 72

BONDING WITH TEENS... 72

CHAPTER 5

ENCOURAGE MORE, CRITICIZE LESS 73

Teens Need Proper Encouragement 73
Proper Encouragement.. 74
The Keep it R.E.A.L. Concept 76
Criticizing/Discouraging Comments: 87
TAKE AWAY POINT... 91

CHAPTER 6

REINVENT YOURSELF 93

Become an Empathy-Driven Parent............................... 93
KNOWLEDGE IS THE EQUALIZER................................. 100
How Does Empathy-Driven Parenting Work.................... 104

CONCLUSION.. 134

RESOURCES 136

ABOUT THE AUTHOR.. 140

Gifting Empathy

⟞⟝⟞◆⟝⟞⟝

I n recent years, teen development and behavior has
been identified as one of the most challenging
public health issues facing society. Due to high
rates of gang participation, violence, bullying, drug use
and pregnancy among teens, parents, teachers, mentors,
mental health professionals and federal and state
agencies are devoted to helping teens successfully
resolve hardships they encounter. Society's growing
obsession with teens has led to millions of dollars spent
to develop and implement programs that focus on
helping teens become productive members of society. A
majority of teen-centered and mentoring programs focus
on helping youth cope with or avoid negative life
challenges such as teen pregnancy, gang involvement,
illegal drug use and school dropouts. A great deal of time
and money is spent teaching youth healthy life skills.

While I believe and agree that teen-centered
programs are important and needed, I also believe that

teen-centered programs are not as successful as they could be because *youth do not raise themselves.* As a result of participating in teen-centered programs, youth learn certain coping skills but then return to their parents or guardians who may not understand or know how to reinforce what their teens have learned. In the earlier part of my career as a psychotherapist, I primarily provided therapy to teenagers who were struggling to cope with a variety of social and psychological issues. From my work, I learned that teens who felt understood were more receptive to feedback and guidance. In contrast, teens who felt misunderstood were more closed-minded and oppositional. As I listened to their stories about their challenges, I learned that many teens behaved inappropriately because they did not believe that their parents or other adults understood or cared about their thoughts or feelings. They often complained about adults' lack of interest in trying to understand them. As I approached parents to share their teens' feelings and concerns, I was often met with defensiveness and frustration. Some parents would say, "I did not act like that when I was a teen" or "my oldest child did not act like that, either. I don't understand why this child is so different and difficult. I do everything I can to make life easy for all of my children."

After many years of listening to parents' frustration and comparing their teen to other teens, I began to develop a better understanding of the parent-teen conflict. As a result of having heartfelt conversations with thousands of parents over the past fifteen years as a psychotherapist, I truly believe that most parents have their teens' best interest at heart and will do whatever it takes to help them to become successful in life.

As I continue to talk with parents in therapy, seminars and youth programs across the nation, I am saddened by the fact that a large percentage of parents have conflicting relationships with their teens because they do not understand their teens and/or lack knowledge about how to bond with them. Most parents seek answers or solutions to resolve or stop their teens' behavioral problems, but often do not inquire about causes or reasons for their teens' behavior. The more that I explore and discuss the parent-teen conflict in therapy and seminars, the more I find that one of the most fundamental problems is associated with a lack of understanding demonstrated by parents who often possess a non-empathic parenting approach or style.

With this in mind, I decided to spend more time in therapy and seminars educating parents about what it means to be empathic toward their teens. Empathy, defined as the ability to understand and identify with others by seeing the world from their point of view, is not an easy task for many parents. Therefore, I encourage parents to put themselves in their teens' shoes. For parents who have difficulty with demonstrating empathy, I encourage them to reflect on their own teen years, focusing on thoughts and feelings that surfaced during and after interacting with their parents or guardians.

Gifting Empathy is a basic parenting approach I developed to teach parents how to understand, influence and bond with their teens by giving them the gift of compassion. The philosophy of *Gifting Empathy* centers on the belief that it is impossible to connect with anyone, especially teens, if you cannot envision yourself in their shoes and offer compassion. *Gifting Empathy* is a compassion and empowerment approach to parenting. While solution-oriented parenting approaches are designed to help parents address and correct teens' behavior, compassion-oriented parenting approaches such as *Gifting Empathy* are designed to help parents teach compassion and gain insight into their teens' behavior by demonstrating empathy. Empathy is an indispensable life skill needed to care for and love others in a healthy manner. Healthy relationships in any setting are based on individuals' abilities to be empathic.

In order to successfully embrace and practice empathy, parents learn how to implement and apply guidelines from my Five-Step Empathy Model:

1. Apply the Golden Rule
2. Suspend Judgment
3. Focus on Emotional Distress
4. Validate Emotions
5. Resolve Emotional Distress

Parents who learn the *Gifting Empathy* approach in psychotherapy, webinars and workshops are also encouraged to reflect on their teens' developmental foundation before attempting to bond or connect with them. They learn to engage in self-reflection in order to develop a better understanding of the mindset and emotional state of their teens.

This book was developed to serve as your personal guide and provides a detailed overview of the concepts and skills parents are taught in therapy and seminars nationwide. This book is not a "one-size-fits-all" approach to parenting. Therefore, I encourage you to apply what you feel is appropriate and applicable to your parent-teen situation. Furthermore, this book is not intended to provide all the answers or solutions to resolving your parent-teen conflict, but it offers one of the most effective resolutions – *Gifting Empathy*.

In its most fundamental nature *Gifting Empathy* is a strategic parenting guide that will help you understand, influence and bond with teens who are participating in a *War* that they did not solely create. Make no mistake; we are at war with our teens. *War* is defined as a state of conflict or hostility between different groups that occurs due to dissimilar views regarding specific conditions or circumstances. Due to advances in technology and the unfortunate rise in teen drug use, pregnancy, bullying, gang participation, sexual promiscuity and violence, conflict between parents and teens is at an all-time high. It is not uncommon to hear teens express different views than their parents when discussing complicated social issues such as sexual identity or activity, drug use, violence, appropriateness of music and how to cope with bullying. Unfortunately, teens are chastised and met with disapproval for having different views or participating in potentially harmful social activities. In my opinion, today's teenagers are often treated similarly to veterans who fought in the Vietnam War.

Most of us have either heard or read about the Vietnam War and how the veterans were treated after they returned home from fighting. They were greeted with hostility and very little empathy as they attempted to reintegrate into society. Many veterans were treated unjustly and were rejected as heroes because a large percentage of society felt that the war was meaningless. The Vietnam conflict was perceived to be a total failure because America withdrew, and the blame was directed primarily toward the veterans who fought and little attention was directed toward the politicians who decided to go to war in the first place.

History tells us that the Vietnam War was a failure, not because the veterans failed, but because those in leadership roles were not knowledgeable about themselves, their allies or their enemies. America learned a life-costing and expensive lesson from the Vietnam War – *no war or conflict can be won without proper knowledge, preparation and strategizing.*

With this in mind, we cannot allow or afford to have history repeat itself. Many veterans turned to drugs due to the trauma they experienced and the hostility they faced upon returning home. The overwhelming amount of rejection veterans experienced from being misunderstood, judged and demoralized contributed to the development of psychiatric conditions and self-destructive behavior making it difficult for many of them to readjust. Unfortunately, a large percentage of today's

Vietnam veterans are mentally and emotionally unstable, homeless or institutionalized. Are any of the abovementioned issues relevant to today's teens?

As parents and leaders, your teens depend on you to nurture and protect them, not fix them. Your success rests not only on your ability to learn and apply disciplinary interventions, but also on your ability to correctly analyze the cause of your parent-teen conflict. Understanding how your teen thinks and feels is critical if you desire to provide him or her with the emotional, intellectual and social support needed to ensure that he or she succeeds in life. To successfully resolve your parent-teen conflict and develop a better understanding of your teen, you must take time to get to know yourselves and your teen, and utilize available resources such as this parenting guide on a regular basis.

This book was written specially to assist parents like you who may feel powerless, discouraged or unequipped to resolve their parent-teen conflict. It provides parents with process-oriented tools needed to succeed. After observing hundreds of parents successfully apply the *Gifting Empathy* parenting approach in therapy and seminars, I am confident that you will have similar success in building a trusting and lasting relationship with your teen.

As you implement the *Gifting Empathy* parenting approach, remember that success can be determined by both process and outcome. Be patient, embrace the challenge, recognize and praise change, remain optimistic, and don't forget that the greatest gift that you can give your teen is the gift of empathy

.

PART ONE

UNDERSTANDING TEENS

CHAPTER 1

Must We Forget

Parents Just Don't Understand

At some point during those chaotic years between age twelve and eighteen, most of us experienced an array of emotions ranging from uncertainty, confusion, sadness and depression to excitement, courageousness, confidence and occasional happiness. At times, we thought that we were invincible and nothing could stop us from doing what we felt like doing, and sometimes we felt insecure and vulnerable. During these turbulent years, our relationship with our parents was beginning to change. Our willingness to be obedient was typically based on our mood or what we thought we could get away with. As we approached twelve years of age and ventured into our "grown up" stage of life, most of us felt that we had earned the right to be more independent and to make our own decisions. For example, I remember staying out past my curfew one night and when I walked through the door, I heard my mother say, "If you think you can come and go as you please then you can start paying rent. I am not obligated to put a roof over your head or food in your mouth. There are rules and everyone under the age of twenty-one who lives in this household will follow them." Does this sound familiar?

I quickly realized that my mother was not going to allow me to be the "man" that I needed to be at twelve-years-old. I felt that her sole purpose in life was to prevent me from leaving her nest and tinting my image as being the "man." I was convinced that my mother had no idea what it meant to be twelve years old. I felt like my life was just beginning and she was trying to ruin it intentionally.

My goal at that point was to prove to my mother that I could take care of myself. Although I did not have a job and barely knew anything about life, I was convinced that I could hold my own and survive based on my own intelligence. I knew I had what it took to survive and to be the man because other women (female peers) believed in me and never questioned my manhood. In addition, my homeboys had more freedom than I did, despite the fact that I was more responsible than they were. I felt victimized because my mother was tripping - she truly did not understand that I was the "man."

Normal Teen Development - *Self-Discovery*

No matter how smart you think your teen is, remember that he or she is still a teen. What does this mean? *Life experience has a way of teaching us things that verbal instruction cannot.* When talking with your teen, keep in mind that he or she is probably struggling with **self-discovery** and developing a sense of autonomy. Their willingness and ability to follow instructions is not solely based on their learned ideas or understanding about what is right or wrong, but their desire to test their own thinking and reasoning skills.

The pursuit of autonomy or independence drives or influences most teen behavior. Teens definitely possess the ability to think logically, but frequently make decisions that are emotional in nature. Your teen might experiment with his or her life and others when in emotional distress or to just simply to test his or her cognitive ability or capacity. During this exploratory process, your teen is likely to become defensive when his or her ideas are challenged regardless of whether he or she believes that they are right or wrong.

Most parents do not do cope well in the midst of such illogical behavior and often ask, "How can I understand or be open to dealing with this inappropriate and irrational behavior?" The answer to this question is simple. I inform parents that *self-discovery* is a normal developmental task that all teens struggle with it. I also remind parents that self-discovery is just as painful for some teens as it is for their parents and I challenge parents to think about their own teen years.

Must We Forget

Large percentages of today's parents respond to and treat their teens as if they are aliens. Some of you operate as if you cannot relate to irrational thinking and behavior. Some parents venture into adulthood and have difficulty recognizing and confessing that they were once teens who did not have it all together. This is exactly why introspection or self-reflection is important. Introspection or self-reflection is the ability to gain insight into one's self by examining one's own thoughts and feelings. As parents and mature adults, some of us have learned the importance of processing our emotions and making healthy decisions, but must we forget how we felt, thought and behaved as teens?

Self-reflection

There are different ways to gain insight about one's past behavior, thoughts and/or feelings. Some people talk with their parents, grandparents or other family members while others engage in self-reflection activities. Despite the method, the goal is to examine and explore your thoughts and feelings in order to grow personally and to develop a better understanding of your teen years. I encourage you to do what works for you; self-reflection works best for me. Here is an experience I recall about my teen years:

Growing up in the inner city of St. Louis, Missouri was not easy. Violence, police brutality and drug distribution was widespread. Gangs such as the Cripps and Bloods ruled the streets. It was not unusual for innocent individuals to be shot or murdered for simply wearing gang colors (red, blue, tan, etc.) in the wrong neighborhood. By the time I reached age fourteen, I had witnessed eight shootings, four police beatings and saw two dead bodies while passing murder scenes on my way home from school. My neighborhood was filled with two groups of young boys: those who hung out, gang banged and sold drugs and those who played sports and tried to avoid trouble. Most teens attempted to do both, but were rarely successful. Given the rampage of violence in the neighborhood, my mother often told me not to hang out with guys who sold or used drugs, stole cars, participated in gang activity or behaved inappropriately. She reminded me that if I hung around people who did bad things I could end up in jail, hurt or dead.

In my infinite wisdom at age fourteen, I thought I knew more than my mother. On a daily basis, I hung out with several guys on one of the most dangerous streets in the neighborhood. We fantasized about driving nice cars like the drug dealers drove. We were also addicted to the energy we felt by observing the heavy traffic and multiple personalities (drug users, dealers, etc.). Hanging out was cool and we earned respect from the older thugs in the hood.

One Saturday evening, while hanging out in front of a drug house with the guys, I spotted the police approaching and to my surprise, they jumped out of their cars and surrounded the house. Out of shock, I took off running and ran through the house next to the drug house. As I exited through the back door, police pointed guns and shouted, "Get down on the ground and don't move." This was the real deal. I was handcuffed, placed in the police paddy wagon with the drug dealers and transported to the local jail station. Once inside the jail station, I was told to take my shoestrings out of my shoes and to remove my belt. I was then escorted to a holding cell that was very dark and cold.

The whole experience screwed me up emotionally. I knew that I was in too deep as I set on the metal bedframe feeling terrified. My body was numb and feelings of terror and uncertainty filled my mind and soul. I attempted to suppress my emotions because I did not want to appear horrified, but my emotions intensified as I listened to the police celebrate and boast about conducting a successful drug raid. One of the policemen said, "We arrested several old guys and a few young boys. Everything went as planned and nobody got hurt."

As I sat in the cell, my mind backtracked and I could not stop thinking about what my mother told me about hanging around "bad" people. I was terrified and believed that I was going to spend a significant amount of time in jail because I was in the wrong place at the wrong time. Several hours passed before a couple of police came to check on me and the other prisoners. As they approached my holding cell, a female officer said, "We should let this young man go. I saw him run out of the house opposite of the one we raided." Her fellow officer asked, "Are you sure?" She answered, "Yes." Within thirty minutes, I was released. Walking away from the jail station was one of the happiest moments in my life, but I was still traumatized.

Upon returning home, my mother said, "I heard that you were taken to the jail station and I want you to know that I was not going to come and get you. You do not listen and I keep telling you that a hard head makes a soft behind. You will learn one day to listen to me when I tell you something."

Listening to my mother was troublesome because she never asked me how I felt. I knew that she was upset and disappointed, but I was still shocked and hurt by the fact that she did not appear to care about my emotional well-being. She always told me that two wrongs do not make a right, so I was looking for comfort in my time of emotional distress even though I did wrong. I tried to make sense of the situation by assuming that she was treating me like an adult because I had made my own decision. I felt confused, frustrated and did not know how to respond to my mother's reaction. After this unfortunate exchange with my mother, I convinced myself to believe that my mother was more concerned about my willingness to follow her instructions than she was with understanding me. At that point, I decided that I would not share how I felt because it did not matter, especially if I was wrong. This began a process of non-self-disclosure, especially if I felt that I was going to be chastised.

This was one of many encounters where I truly felt disappointed and rejected because my mother never asked me why I wanted to hang out with those guys. I wanted to tell her that I felt cool overall, but also hung out with those guys because I felt sorry for them. Unlike me, they did not have anyone who cared about or attempted to discipline them. I was connected, not because I wanted to be like them, but because they knew what it felt like not to be heard or accepted, especially when adults were not being pleased. I felt that they could relate to me and me to them. As I learned more about each of those guys on a daily basis, I liked them even more. Our bond was built on respect and familiarity; I, like them, believed that our parents just didn't understand.

Learning from Self-Reflection

The reason I shared my story was not to bash my mother, but to illustrate the importance of engaging in self-reflection in order to begin the process of understanding the developmentally limited mindset, behavior and emotional reasoning that is common among most teens. If you are extremely lucky, your teen will obey your every demand. However, if you are like most parents I work and interact with, I recommend that you fasten your seatbelt as your child approaches his or her teen years. As a co-pilot on his or her expedition, you will experience turbulence as your teen travels the path of personal discovery and searches for independence. As you travel beside your teen, I encourage you to take a moment to reflect on your own teen years. If you think long and hard enough, I am confident that you can recall a moment or two during your teen years where you felt misunderstood and/or emotionally abandoned by your parents or guardians. I challenge you not to be the parent who suffers from amnesia when it comes to interacting with your teen.

The quickest and most convenient way to begin the process of understanding and bonding with your teen is to think about yourself. Teens will not always make the right decisions, but they will always look for support and understanding. Some will display inappropriate behavior when they are disappointed while others might simply withdraw emotionally. Either way, you have to contend with a problem. Most teens are struggling with challenges and/or questions centered on sexuality, drugs, peer pressure, relationships, and future employment. They typically spend a considerable amount of time and energy searching for answers or solutions to things that consume or worry them. *If teens cannot or do not get answers from adults, they will turn to media outlets and/or their peers.* Anyone who interacts with them on a regular basis will likely witness an array of thoughts and emotions as they process and struggle to develop coping mechanisms to help them during their most challenging developmental stage - *Self-discovery.*

I have empathy for you and understand your challenge as parents. On a daily basis, you are responsible for nurturing, teaching, providing for and protecting your teen, while also trying to take care of yourself and other family members. It is normal to feel frustrated and discouraged, but you cannot afford to lose sight of what it felt like to be a teen. Do you remember how you saw the world through the invincible and stubborn eyes of a teen before you ventured into adulthood?

I challenge you to revisit the teen in you. As a teen, did you search for meaning in your life, fight for independence or express a desire to have privacy and respect? Did you have a desire to bond with or be liked by your peers? Did you take risks although you knew right from wrong? Did you question or feel the urge to question your parents? Did you believe that your relationship with your peers was more important than or as equally important as your relationship with your parents? Did your parents or other adults tell you that you behaved irrationally or inappropriately occasionally? If you answered "yes" to one or more of the questions listed above, you are one step closer to developing a better understanding of your teen.

Benefit of Engaging in Self-Reflection

You can understand your teen by reflecting and equipping yourself with proper knowledge. Through self-reflection, everyone has the ability to grow. *As you explore your past, you will be freed from the rigid and insensitive views that oppressed you as a teen.* This does not mean that you will not continue to face challenges or occasionally get frustrated as a parent, because teens are liberated to use their *Free Will* as they see fit, but you will be better equipped to cope with your teen's *Self-discovery* phase. Remember that your purpose as a parent is to teach, uplift and nurture your teen, but do not become obsessed with the need to control him or her. Furthermore, do not compare his or her life experiences to yours. Times have changed and most teens cannot relate to social problems that occurred two or three decades ago. Keep in mind that your ability to relate to your teen will strongly influence the nature of your parent-teen relationship. If you do nothing else as a parent, take a moment to reflect on your own teen years, and then use that information as a guide to connect with your teen in an empathic manner. Believe me- the emotional synergy and peace of mind you will feel will be worth the effort, and your teen will appreciate the empathy that manifests as a result.

TAKE AWAY POINT

Understanding how teens process mentally and emotionally is the key to understanding them.

QUESTIONS FOR REFLECTION AND PROCESSING

Unfortunately, some of you do not take or make time to reflect on your past, and those who do often use your experience as a gauge to interact with your teen. Below are some basic questions designed to help you reflect on your past. Answering the questions will help you remember what it was like to be a teen and challenge you to think about the personal, interpersonal and social tribulations your teen currently faces.

What was your biggest challenge as a teen (peer pressure, strict parents, drug use, partying, hanging out, bullying, sexual activity, fighting, etc.)?

_____

_____

_____

_____

_____

_____

_____

_____

_____

_____

_____

_____

_____

_____

How did you cope?

_____

_____

_____

_____

_____

_____

_____

_____

_____

_____

_____

_____

_____

_____

_____

_____

_____

How would you feel or behave if you were a teen today?

_____

_____

_____

_____

_____

_____

_____

_____

_____

_____

_____

_____

What or who would influence you the most if you were a teen today (T.V., peers, media, parents, etc.)?

_____

_____

_____

_____

_____

_____

_____

_____

_____

_____

_____

_____

_____

_____

_____

_____

_____

How would you cope with teen violence, peer pressure, etc.?

_____

_____

_____

_____

_____

_____

_____

_____

_____

_____

_____

_____

_____

_____

_____

SHARE YOUR ANSWERS WITH YOUR TEEN TO
DETERMINE IF YOUR THOUGHTS or FEELINGS
ARE SIMILAR TO HIS OR HERS

Write the outcome here:

_____
_____
_____
_____
_____
_____
_____
_____
_____
_____
_____
_____

CHAPTER 2

Withhold the Instructions

―――――⬥―――――

Teens Need to Be Heard

As you reflect on your teen years, what upset you the most or contributed to you becoming defensive or withdrawn when your parents or guardians talked to you about your behavior or feelings? Did the conversations begin with, "*Listen to me. I do not want to hear that nonsense. Let me tell you what you need to do…?*" How did you respond? Was your response similar to mine? For me, the moment I heard "*Listen to me…*" or "*Let me…,*" I immediately became defensive and shut down. I knew that I was going to be lectured and if I did not listen, I was going to be punished. As a result, I listened well enough to repeat what was said in case I was asked, "*What did I just say to you?*" However, I rarely processed anything. I repeated content or words, but often did not try to understand their meaning or message.

Conversations with my mother and other adults often began and ended with them telling me how I should think, feel and behave. As I reflect on my relationships with adults, I believe that a great deal of tension was present between us because I did not feel like I was heard or understood. The world I existed in was totally different from theirs. I faced situations that my mother and other adults did not experience as a teen, but my views did not matter because I was too young to understand how the world really worked.

Parents regularly associate teen defensiveness with normal rebellious behavior. However, many parents fail to realize that no one, including mature adults, likes to be told how they should think, feel or behave without being given opportunities to express themselves. In most healthy conversations, two individuals typically exchange views or opinions about a particular topic or issue. Two-way conversations are conducted to make sure that both perspectives are heard and understood.

Two-way conversations are designed to facilitate the development of mutual respect and trust in relationships.

Most teens are frequently told that they should not speak while someone else is speaking, but should respectfully request an opportunity to voice their thoughts afterward. On many occasions, I have observed teens attempting to apply what they were taught, but unfortunately, I do not recall listening to many two-way conversations. Most conversations I observe between parents and teens are usually one-sided. Here are a few examples:

Conversation #1:

Parent: "Your math teacher sent a letter home. I am sick and tired of you acting out in school. You have an opportunity to get a good education and you are too hard-headed to take advantage. You get in trouble one more time, I am going to beat your butt."

Teen: "Can I explain what happened?"

Parent: "I do not have time to listen to your excuses. I read the letter. You need to do what you are told. I did not raise you to be disrespectful. You are going to go back to school and tell your math teacher that you are sorry for disrupting her class. You are so smart and I do not understand why you get in trouble so much. You have no reason to be disruptive. People are just trying to do right by you."

Conversation #2:

Parent: "Your brother told me that you do not like the new shoes I bought you because they are not Air Jordans. He told me that you do not wear them to school."

Teen: "I was going to talk to you about the shoes and explain why I don't like wearing them."

Parent: "Stop! I buy what I can afford. If you want expensive shoes, get a job. Don't be ungrateful. Learn to appreciate things. I did when I was your age."

Conversation #3:

Parent: "Your mother told me that you did not do your chores today. I don't ask much of you, but everybody has to do their part in this house."

Teen: "I was going to come and talk to you."

Parent: "Here we go again. You make everything so difficult. If you just do what is expected there is no need to have discussions about chores. We can talk later; you need to do the chores now."

As reflected above, all three conversations were one-sided and ended with the parents being up two exchanges to their teens' one. The parents' views and positions regarding the issues were very clear and their teens understood them. In all three examples listed above, the teens did not have opportunities to express their thoughts or feelings and walked away from the conversations feeling very angry but knew exactly what the expectations were. It is not unusual for this style of communication to be demonstrated by some parents, especially those who embrace the belief that children should listen and only offer their opinions or views when asked. Unfortunately, this commonly held belief is the underlying reason for most one-way conversations – *parents talk and teens listen.*

From a professional and personal perspective, I have learned the importance of not instructing teens to think, feel or behave without hearing them out. Regardless of how confident or disobedient teens may appear, many experience a variety of conflicting emotions (confidence, sadness, excitement, disappointment, etc.) and in general desire help with understanding and resolving their emotions. In chatting with hundreds of teens, I have learned that it is very frustrating not to be heard. During our discussions teens frequently ask, "Why should I share anything with my parents or other adults if they are just going to tell me what to do?"

Withholding instructions is a difficult task for many parents because you feel that it is your ultimate and sole responsibility to guide, educate and teach your teen. You feel obligated to provide a wealth of information and feel empowered when doing so. While this responsibility is noteworthy and important, you must remember that learning occurs as a result of a two-way dialogue. Without discussion, only the listener acquires new information. However, by engaging in a two-way dialogue, both the speaker and listener can acquire new information. Through the dialectic process, information flows in two directions and both parties have equal opportunities to give and receive information. The two diagrams below reflect typical communication patterns between parents and teens. Which diagram best illustrates how you communicate with your teen?

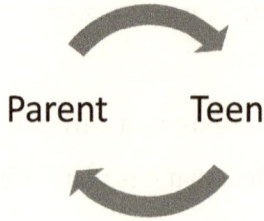

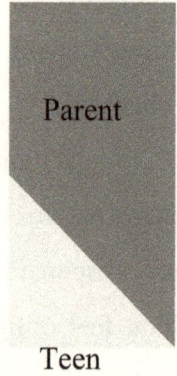

Diagram 1 – Two-way Communication
Diagram 2- One-way Communication

The challenge for most parents is deciding when and what to listen to while interacting with their teens. However, I encourage you to listen to anything that your teen is willing to share with you no matter how ridiculous it might sound. The more your teen talks about his or her life and/or experiences, the better informed you will become as a parent. I often joke with parents in therapy and seminars by telling them that *God created us with two ears and one mouth because He understood the value of listening. He also understood that distressed teens would need to be heard.*

As an experienced psychotherapist, I have learned the value and importance of listening to people, especially teens. Teens, like adults, feel safe and comfortable when they feel they are being heard. Expressing a genuine concern about their emotional and social well-being helps with establishing a safe zone. I have found that teens' safe zones are no different from adults'. Most people do not like feeling vulnerable so they struggle with honestly sharing their feelings. However, if they believe or feel that they will gain something by sharing, they will.

When teens refuse to talk or withdraw, sometimes the problem is that they are afraid that they will not be taken seriously or be heard. It's all too easy for some parents to instruct or offer suggestions than it is to listen to their teens. To this day, I'm convinced that most teens will talk to anyone who makes them feel safe and provides some form of security. The need for emotional safety is a basic human need and when teens' emotional safety needs are met, they are more prone to minimize or reduce their defensiveness. Therefore, if you struggle to understand and connect with your teen, it may be time to reevaluate and readjust your communication style. Perhaps the most important skill needed to understand teens is to withhold instructions. Why is this important? Withholding instructions entails the following benefits for both parents and teens:

> Parents are better informed about their teens' behavioral and emotional issues or concerns.

> Parents establish rapport with their teens by listening.

> Respect is earned and demonstrated by both.

> Parents can provide clearer and more relevant instructions.

> Teens learn the importance of processing emotions.

> Teens' emotional safety needs can be met.

> Two-way communication is facilitated and practiced.

> Teens learn good reasoning and conflict resolution skills.

> Communication channels remain open for future encounters.

In healthy relationships, two-way communication is critical. When parents interact with their teens without instructing them prematurely, communication flows smoothly and all parties normally walk away feeling better. To illustrate how two-way conversations should be conducted between a parent and teen, let's revisit Conversation #1 presented above.

Conversation #1:

Parent: "Your math teacher sent a letter home stating that you have been acting out in her class. Do you want to discuss this?"

Teen: "Yes, I can explain why I have been acting out."

Parent: "I am listening."

Teen: "I finish my work early and I get bored."

Parent: "Why do you get bored? Is the work too easy for you?"

Teen: "Yes, I finish my work and start messing with my classmates."

Parent: "Are there other things you can do in class after you finish?"

Teen: "Yes, the teacher gives extra credit for doing extra math problems."

Parent: "I encourage you to talk to your teacher about getting some extra credit. Also, I will talk to your teacher about the possibility of enrolling you in a more advanced math class."

Teen: "I thought you were going to scream and chastise me."

Parent: "I am not pleased with your behavior because you know better, but I understand that people can get sidetracked and lose focus when they are bored. You should not be afraid to tell me anything. I am not perfect and do not always have all the answers, but I will listen."

As you learn to withhold instructions, you will become a better listener, which in turn will empower you to facilitate two-way communication with your teen. When you acknowledge and openly discuss your teen's thoughts and emotions, your relationship and bond strengthen. Ensuring that you nurture your teen's emotional well-being is equally as important as ensuring that he or she behaves appropriately.

Listening to your teen's views and emotions, even if you do not agree with them, demonstrates your ability to appreciate his or her point of view. Being flexible in your thinking and behavior is critical to being able to understand your teen. However, since some parents struggle with withholding instructions and demonstrating emotional sensitivity when interacting with their teens, the next chapter will help you understand the importance of why *Giving Empathy* parenting is not optional.

God created us with two ears and one mouth

Why do I encourage parents to listen more and instruct less? Listening establishes the foundation for "true" emotional and social bonding. Given this, it is important that you learn to identify and eliminate one-way communication phrases that prevent you from having open discussions with your teen. To assist with this task, I encourage you to become familiar with and learn to distinguish between the one-way and two-way communication phrases listed in the diagram below:

One –Way Phrases   Two-Way Phrases

One –Way Phrases	Two-Way Phrases
Let me Tell You	I am willing to listen
You need to	I am open to what you have say
Do as I tell you	What are you thinking?
Listen to me	Please speak your mind

Remember that nearly all teens will shut down immediately if you start communication by using one-way communication phrases. Such phrases communicate that they do not have an equal right to express their thoughts or emotions. Once you are able to withhold instructions, you'll have better success with understanding your teen.

QUESTIONS FOR REFLECTION AND PROCESSING

Do you believe that it is possible to establish a healthy relationship with your teen?

_____

_____

_____

_____

_____

_____

_____

_____

_____

_____

_____

_____

Do you listen to your teen? Why or Why not?

_____

_____

_____

_____

_____

_____

_____

_____

_____

_____

_____

_____

_____

_____

_____

_____

_____

_____

_____

_____

_____

_____

_____

_____

_____

CHAPTER 3

Spend Time with Your Teen

———————◇———————

Teens Need Attention

Why do some teens go out of their way to be noticed by their parents and peers? According to Abraham Maslow, a renowned psychologist, all humans have five basic needs: physiological, security, social, esteem and self-actualizing. Parents typically address their teen's physiological needs: water and food. Parents also address their teen's safety and security needs: protection from harm and shelter from the environment. However, of all the basic needs presented by Maslow, social needs, which include the need for belonging, love and affection, best describe why some teens go out of their way to be noticed by their parents and peers.

The desire to have companionship and to be accepted is an intense social need that dictates how your teen behaves the majority of the time. He or she will do whatever is required to get attention and will occasionally rely on you to help him or her figure out how to cope with the transformation from childhood to "independent" teen. As he or she strives to achieve independence, he or she will create bonds with peers and rely on them just as much as he or she relies on you. Bonding with peers will occur naturally as your teen shares experiences with like-minded individuals who provide comfort and understanding.

You may feel neglected or slightly jealous as your teen beings to trust and confide in others. You may also struggle to accept that you no longer have "total" influence over your teen's life. Your teen's physical appearance, dress, mannerism, thinking and vocabulary may change based on influence from his peers and media outlets. He may dress or behave differently with the intent of creating an impact and establishing a reputation among peers. During this self-exploration and adjustment period, conflict is likely to occur between you and your teen, especially if you have difficulty meeting his social needs or if you attempt to prevent him from bonding with peers. Be mindful that your teen is exercising his "independent right" when selecting peer acquaintances. If you try to stop this from occurring, you will likely be met with intense hostility. For the most part, all teens will respond aggressively when they perceive that their ability to fulfill their own social needs is being threatened.

You can better understand your teen's deep-felt need to be in control of his life, to belong and to be accepted by paying attention to the self-destructive and risk-taking behavior that he participates in to avoid being ignored. Once you understand and accept that teens crave attention, your ability to understand and influence them will be met with less resistance. However, you must make time to nurture their needs. No matter how much time your teen spends with peers, he will always turn to you for affection and reassurance. In your teen's quest to establish his own identity, develop friendships and cope with moral issues, he will definitely need your help. Will you be available? In most households, both parents work in order to address their teen's physiological and security needs.

Because you are consumed with addressing basic survival needs, you occasionally neglect your teen's social need for attention and affection. Regrettably, this universal problem affects thousands of parent-teen relationships on a daily basis. Many parents, especially single parents, work long hours or two jobs in order to provide for and address their teen's primary needs. As a result of economic hardship or obsession with financial security, some of you have convinced yourself to believe that working is equally as important as spending time with your teen. Like many Americans, you are obsessed with having nice things and financial security. Some of you attempt to compensate for being absent from your teen's life by buying them nice clothes, enrolling them in private schools or sports programs, and providing them with opportunities to experience and do things you could not do as a teen.

As a parent and provider, you make sure that your teen is cared for – fed, housed, clothed, educated and entertained. However, most of you spoil your teen by buying expensive video games, clothing and other insignificant material items in order to meet his or her need for attention. This is problematic and causes conflict more often than not because your teen becomes accustomed to having nice things that occupy his or her attention. Your demand or request to spend time with him or her when you are available will likely be met with resistance. When your teen resists your request to spend time together, do not take it personal or get tied up in power struggles. It is normal for individuals to resist when asked to give up something that is familiar and enjoyable to them. This is why teens appear to be rebellious and defiant most of the time - you place demands or requests for your teen's time when it is convenient for you.

For teens, familiarity and frequency play a major role in determining how and when they bond with others. The more time you spend with your teen, the greater influence you will have. This sounds simple, but I realize that it is not so simplistic.

Balancing your parental and professional responsibilities can be very challenging. Work demands can consume a large percentage of your time. However, your inability to spend quantity time with your teen does not mean that you cannot spend quality time with him or her. In my opinion, you can have a greater influence in your teen's life if you focus on having quality interactions as opposed to quantity interactions.

Quality versus Quantity Time

To influence your teen, you must address and meet his or her need for attention. You can accomplish this task by having meaningful and quality interactions with your teen. I am a fundamental believer in making the most of one's time. During my weekly therapy sessions, I learn more about patients in one hour than their family members do who reside with them on a daily basis. I am capable of establishing such rapport with patients because I express a genuine interest in their emotional well-being. I advise you to do the same with your teen.

As you get to know your teen on an emotional level, you will collect information that will enable you to get to know him or her better. You will also be more likely to see similarities between your teen's needs and yours. Quality interactions with your teen will allow you to influence their thinking and behavior because you will be able to identify with them, relate to them and empathize with them. Nothing is more important than addressing your teen's need for attention. Providing for your teen is a major part of your parental responsibility, and I argue that if you simply recognize and embrace the importance of spending quality time with your teen, you might find that it is not too difficult to influence him or her.

I know that you love your teen and will do whatever you can to make him or her happy. Therefore, I ask that you do not lose sight of the fact that we are living in an era where your teen needs your time and attention just as much as he or she needs your love and gifts. Telling your teen that you love him or her and giving them nice things is not enough. As a matter of fact, love and possession of material items has little impact on how individuals behave, especially if nothing is done to stimulate or nurture the love in their hearts. True companionship requires emotional bonding that occurs through interaction – not by giving or receiving material items.

How many times have you heard someone say, "Money cannot buy love?" Do you agree with this saying? I do! Unfortunately, wealthy parents experience just as much hardship and tension with their teens as do middle class and poor parents. The need for attention pertains to all human beings regardless of their economic or financial status. Do you remember the Menendez Brothers? They were convicted and jailed for murdering their wealthy parents in 1989. As you hear about past and current reports of violence exhibited by teens from wealthy, middle class and poor families, what comes to mind? What do you think is the problem?

Most family therapists would agree that teens are more prone to engage in self-destructive, dangerous and violent behavior if their needs for safety, affection and belonging are not adequately addressed or satisfied. To support this assertion, the following excerpt from my book, "A Black Man's Worth: Conqueror and Head of Household" provides a brief overview of the emotional distress I experienced as a teen who did not receive adequate attention:

"I grew up viewing myself and other Black males negatively. I thought all Black men were sadistic because they did horrible things that were destructive to themselves and others. While riding down the street with my mother and older brother, my mother's ex-boyfriend shot at the car, and I was hit in the arm. He was angry because my mother ended their relationship. At this point in my life, I was already miserable and numb to emotional pain, so the shooting did not significantly affect me. *I believed wholeheartedly that my life was dispensable. I hoped for the best, but expected the worst.*

Life was filled with disappointment. The man who was supposed to be my father told me that he was not because I made him angry. With all the madness and destruction around me, I found peace in learning how to dissociate from my surroundings to feel safe. I dreamed about being a doctor who healed the sick. I did whatever I could to maintain a positive view of myself as a Black male. However, this coping mechanism slowly faded as

I was reminded daily of my reality. There were no doctors walking the streets of my neighborhood. I could not identify with the lifestyle of a doctor. However, I was very familiar with the lifestyle of drug dealers, gangsters, and blue-collar workers. I was confused and did not understand why my lifestyle did not resemble the lifestyle of white children I watched on television. They were protected from violence, received suitable education, were supported emotionally, mentored when faced with life challenges, and their parents were granted equal and viable employment opportunities. My mind drifted regularly. It was difficult for me to distinguish between fantasy and reality.

I often fantasized about living in a community where I could walk out my door and not worry about being shot, offered drugs, or jumped by bullies. I fantasized about living where I could receive a suitable education. I fantasized about having positive male role models who could help me cope with life challenges. I fantasized about having a father present who could help my mother take care of us and relieve her financial burden. As my fantasies grew, so did my awareness of my reality. I lived in a one-bedroom apartment in the ghetto with my mother, younger brother, and sister. I fought to survive and protect myself from bullies. I attended schools that were substandard and was educated by teachers who were underpaid and burnt-out. I looked to my peers to help me cope with life challenges because I did not have positive adult male role models. My teen years were difficult for me. I struggled with my reality. Again, I began to question my existence. *Does my life have meaning?*

I was bitter as a teenager and engaged in behaviors that were familiar to me. I exploited young girls sexually for self-gratification and used violence against those who threatened my "manhood" or ability to survive. I did not care about my life and had little concern for others. At times, I even struggled to love family members and friends who did not express love for me, at least not in a way that I could appreciate. As I experienced personal hardships, my bitterness grew, and I eventually turned to the streets for understanding and acceptance. My peers were struggling with similar hardships and understood my misery. They also questioned their existence and desperately sought to understand meaning in their lives. We found comfort in each other's despair. We wanted nice things and security, but most importantly, we wanted to be loved, understood, and accepted. We developed a brotherhood built on pain, misery, and anguish. Life in the "hood" was intolerable at times, so we promised to support each other financially, physically, and emotionally. We observed others, studied our environment, and learned to identify weak individuals. We targeted young girls who displayed an inferiority complex, and brothers who could not 'bang.'

The behavior I engaged in was commonly practiced. I did not feel guilty. Experiencing and inflicting pain was normal. How could I find it within myself to love, respect, and treat others justly when my life was filled with fear, disappointment, and pain? I was a hurt teen trying to find "*meaning*" in my life."

After reading the excerpt above, I hope you understand why you should spend as much time with your teen as possible. You cannot stop your teen from experiencing life, but you can help him understand it. You must know that you can understand your teen's thinking and behavior by being involved in his life. Spending quality time with your teen has benefits: 1) You can influence his behavior by helping with the development of empathy; this is important because empathic teens are better equipped to resist painful urges; and 2) You can identify if your teen is troubled or just seeks trouble.

As I point out in the next chapter, it is important to be able to distinguish between "Troubled Teens vs. Trouble-Seeking Teens" because doing so will give you a better understanding of how to respond to your teen. Remember - *Behind every action, there is an associated emotion.*

TAKE AWAY POINT

> *The ability to understand your teen is impossible if you do not spend time with him or her.*

QUESTIONS FOR REFLECTION AND PROCESSING

Who and what influences your teen the most?

_____

_____

_____

_____

_____

_____

_____

_____

_____

_____

_____

_____

What challenges do you think you will encounter as you request to spend quality time with your teen?

_____

_____

_____

_____

_____

_____

_____

_____

_____

_____

_____

_____

What typically prevents you from spending quality time with your teen?

_____

_____

_____

_____

_____

_____

_____

_____

_____

_____

_____

_____

What personal and professional adjustments will you make to ensure that you spend quality time with your teen?

_____

_____

_____

_____

_____

_____

_____

_____

_____

_____

_____

_____

CHAPTER 4

Troubled Teens

How to Identify and Respond To Troubled Teens

As discussed in the previous chapter, all teens crave attention and often do whatever it takes to get attention. Therefore, parents are typically consumed by what appears to be a never-ending mission to address and resolve attention-seeking behavior. Some teen attention-seeking behaviors occur due to emotional disturbances, while others occur because of interpersonal or environmental disturbances. Too often, many parents attempt to address all attention-seeking behavior with a punisher's mindset, but unfortunately do not realize that some attention-seeking behavior should not be addressed with punishment.

In working with hundreds of teens over the years, I have learned that all teens seek and require some form of attention and typically fall into two categories: troubled teens or trouble-seeking teens. Understanding whether your teen is a troubled teen or trouble-seeking teen is the next step in resolving your frustration and improving your relationship with him or her. Once you identify which category your teen falls into, you will be better equipped to influence his or her behavior and help him or her develop healthy coping skills. Your teen might only need an empathic ear and a compassionate response. Understanding what your teen needs and knowing why he behaves the way he does can help you to respond appropriately.

Troubled Teens

Unfortunately, a large percentage of today's teens are considered troubled. It is common for troubled teens to act out or seek attention because they are struggling emotionally. It is also not uncommon for troubled teens to suffer from psychological disorders such as

Depression, Post-traumatic Stress Disorder (PTSD), Attention Deficit Hyperactive Disorder (ADHD), Eating Disorders and Generalized Anxiety Disorder (GAD). According to results from the National Comorbidity Survey released in 2010, at least 50 percent of all teens have experienced enough symptoms to meet criteria for at least one psychiatric diagnosis by their eighteenth birthday.

Identifying Troubled Teens

Troubled Teens Need Affection, Not Punishment

Today's teens are faced with a multitude of personal and societal challenges ranging from self-discovery during puberty to effectively coping with gang violence, bullying and other destructive ills. Despite their views or beliefs about being invincible, I have found that a large percentage of teens suffer from depression and other psychiatric conditions. With this in mind, it is important that you learn how to differentiate troubled teens from trouble-seeking teens. Identifying whether or not your teen is troubled is critical because it will influence how you respond to him. Here are some typical psychological and behavioral characteristics of troubled teens:

1. Struggles with feelings of sadness, depression and worthlessness
2. Lacks enthusiasm and motivation
3. Withdraws from friends or family
4. Reports hopelessness and helplessness
5. Easily irritated
6. Displays anger frequently or inappropriately
7. Suffers from low self-esteem
8. Overly sensitive to criticism, failure or rejection
9. Performs poorly in school due to psychiatric condition
10. Uses alcohol or other substance to cope with life stressors
11. Engages in reckless behavior due to psychological hostility
12. Has difficulty concentrating

Troubled Teens Who Seek Trouble

Troubled teens who seek trouble are typically defined as thrill-seekers and risk-takers. They look for trouble and may or may not suffer from or meet criteria for any psychiatric condition. Their quest to cause chaos is often associated with feelings of boredom, lack of stimulation or the need to be popular. They find pleasure in being different. It not uncommon for them to rebel and gravitate toward individuals who use drugs, bully others or engage in reckless behavior to prove that they are cool. Participation in destructive activities such as drug and alcohol abuse, unprotected sex, gang participation, drinking and driving, and defying authority figures sends a clear message to peers and others that says, "I am cool."

The need to be recognized and accepted by peers may overshadow the need for safety or parental approval. They welcome negative attention and are stimulated by the responses of individuals who disapprove of their behavior. They embrace being different and part of the in-crowd with pride and confidence. Teens who seek trouble are more likely to become oppositional and/or aggressive if their desire to join forces with peers who represent what they want is denied

Identifying Troubled Teens Who Seek Trouble

Trouble-Seeking Teens Demand Attention

Due to the destructive nature of their behavior, it is not unusual for trouble-seeking teens to be labeled with psychological disorders such as Conduct Disorder, Oppositional Defiant Disorder or Disruptive Behavior Disorder NOS. The demand for attention and willingness to engage in troublesome behavior makes it very difficult for parents and other authority figures to cope with teens who demonstrate trouble-seeking behavior. Nevertheless, parents must familiarize themselves with the psychological and behavioral characteristics of teens who seek trouble in order to approach them and address their behavior appropriately. If you struggle to determine or identify whether or not your teen is a trouble-seeking teen, use the following criteria:

1. Finds pleasure with being a member of in-crowds
2. Lacks enthusiasm and motivation as an individual
3. Demands attention from friends or family
4. Seeks reassurance, but appears to be confident
5. Easily aroused and motivated by negative stimuli
6. Can be needy and pushy
7. Bonds with individuals who think and act similarly
8. Seeks praise and acceptance from anyone for attention
9. Performs poorly in school due to clowning around
10. Uses alcohol or other substances to impress others
11. Engages in reckless behavior to get a thrill
12. Has difficulty with controlling self if the center of attention

Responding to Troubled Teens

Troubled teens typically do not seek trouble because it often finds them. One of the greatest challenges that troubled teens face is their inability to advocate for themselves and get the help they need. This challenge is widespread among troubled teens because they usually have difficulty with recognition and acceptance of their emotional distress. The desire to be "normal" like other teens typically inhibits troubled teens from accepting and coping with their psychiatric condition in a healthy manner. Given that they are already struggling emotionally, it is imperative that they are surrounded by caring and empathy-driven parents. To help your teen cope with his emotional distress in an effective manner, use the following suggestions as response guidelines:

- Inquire about your teen's emotional distress and seek professional help (if warranted).
- Provide support by showing empathy, not sympathy. Feeling sorry for your teen does not help with acceptance.
- Do not become an enabler by making excuses for your teen's inappropriate attention-seeking behavior due to his emotional distress.

- Help your teen process his emotions and feelings. Allow him to express his distress, but encourage healthy behavior.

- Remind your teen of his strengths and encourage him to do things that reinforce the development of positive self-esteem.

- Discipline your teen, but make sure that you let your teen know that you are disciplining him because of his behavior and not because of his emotional distress.

While it is important to identify if your teen is misbehaving or seeking attention because he is troubled, this can be a very intimidating task. As you attempt to identify and understand your troubled teen, you may receive multiple explanations regarding his attention-seeking behavior. For example, many social science researchers suggest that human behavior and development can be influenced by a number of different factors such as genetic temperament, environmental and interpersonal influences, and learned behavior. I mention the latter factors because most parents spend a significant amount of time trying to figure out why their teen is misbehaving instead of trying to understand how to identify and understand emotional distress that might contribute to or cause attention-seeking behavior. If your teen appears to be in emotional distress, seek professional assistance immediately. Identification and understanding of emotional distress is critical because it can help you respond to your teen in a more productive and helpful manner.

Solutions for Dealing with Troubled and Trouble-Seeking Teens:

1) Schedule regular sit-down meetings to discuss behavioral issues or the need for change when things are going well. This will make it easier to talk when things are not going so well. Calm conversations are easier to have than intense and anger-filled conversations.

2) Make it a regular habit to have follow up meetings.

3) Have accountability talks with your teen. Teach them the importance of accepting responsibility for their behavior.

4) Enforce consequences

> *Living in reality is better than fantasy because it prepares you to respond in a realistic manner.*

Do you have a clear understanding of love and how it works? Do you fantasize, but fail to see relationships for what they are? Do you believe that relationships require work? Why or Why not?

_____

_____

_____

_____

_____

PART TWO

BONDING WITH TEENS

CHAPTER 5

Encourage More, Criticize Less

———————⊰≈⬦≈⊱———————

Teens Need Proper Encouragement

Understanding how to properly encourage your teen is critical to getting along with him and minimizing tension in your relationship. Most teens engage in rebellious behavior when they feel like they are being overly or wrongly criticized. Criticizing your teen's decisions and behavior will often result in misbehavior, self-doubt and negative interactions. Encouragement, on the other hand, will often promote good behavior, self-confidence and positive interactions.

Your ability to have a good relationship with your teen is strongly influenced by your capacity to provide proper encouragement. With this in mind, it is imperative that you learn the importance of how to encourage your teen properly. The ability to effectively encourage others is a skill that cannot be learned without training and understanding. I often remind parents that encouragement should not solely be offered in order to get their teens to comply with their requests or suggestions. Encouragement should be offered to provide support with the intent of letting your teen know that you have confidence in his ability to problem solve and correct problems. Your job as a parent is to **back-up** or support your teen, not control him.

Proper Encouragement

Proper encouragement is best described as encouragement that is suitable, appropriate and effective. This means that encouragement or support should be communicated in a manner in which it can be received and processed as being helpful. If you provide encouragement to your teen and it is met with resistance or frustration, you should reexamine your approach. Remember that the primary purpose of providing proper encouragement is to help your teen feel good or confident about carrying out or performing tasks. At times, you might find it difficult to distinguish between what your teen needs or wants from you. When you find yourself struggling to distinguish between the two, step back and ask yourself the following questions: 1) What needs to be accomplished?; 2) What is the best way to accomplish it?; 3) What works?; and 4) What does not work?

After asking yourself these questions, hopefully you will conclude that the best way to answer the questions and offer proper encouragement to your teen is to solicit his input. Proper encouragement requires that you solicit input about what is best from your teen. This process-orientated approach will allow your teen to make decisions and also enable you to provide guidance that your teen will and can embrace. Soliciting input from your teen will highlight your ability to recognize and accept his decisions and efforts, which in turn can lead to the development of mutual respect.

Providing proper encouragement is critical to developing positive, healthy and respectful relationships. However, parents who criticize more than they encourage will facilitate the development of insecurity and confusion in their teens, thus contributing to ongoing parent-teen conflict. To help you avoid this pitfall and understand the importance of providing proper encouragement, I developed the Keep it R.E.A.L. concept and have found it to be instrumental in helping parents minimize their teens' rebellious behavior by providing proper encouragement.

The Keep it R.E.A.L. Concept

Assisting your teen with developing a strong sense of self while also maintaining mutual respect can be challenging. Given this, I developed the Keep it R.E.A.L. concept as a tool to help you provide proper encouragement to your teen and develop the mutual respect that you desire in your parent-teen relationship. Your ability to keep it R.E.A.L. with your teen will determine whether your relationship will be one of acceptance and respect or rejection and disrespect. The R.E.A.L. Concept is articulated as:

R – *Realistic* approach
E – Rational *Expectations*

A – Positive *Attitude*

L – *Love* unconditionally

The "R"

The **R** encourages you to approach situations with your teen in a **Realistic** manner. It is important to express an awareness of things as they really are but use sound judgment and demonstrate empathy. Seek to understand the source of your teen's problems before you attempt to address or solve them.

Realize that your ability to influence your teen will occur as a result of providing proper encouragement. Always be willing to demonstrate respect and support for your teen. Encouragement is vital in parent-teen relationships and you can demonstrate this by leading and guiding empathically.

Unfortunately, many parents believe that they can talk down to or criticize their teens and get positive results. This approach to parenting is not realistic or very effective because sound judgment and empathy is not being demonstrated. Parents who use this parenting method often do not approach situations realistically. They fail to provide proper encouragement because they do not view their teens as responsible or competent individuals capable of making good decisions. Instead, they criticize with the hope that their teens will do better if they feel bad. While this approach might invoke a behavioral change or response, it will not invoke a strong sense of self or feeling of being independent or in control.

Be mindful that most teens are struggling with the question of "Who am I?" and are sensitive to criticism. If you want your teen to make healthy and positive decisions and evolve into a confident adult, you must approach him in a nonjudgmental and empathic manner. Do not criticize your teen for his effort or assume that you know what your teens needs or wants without soliciting his input. Seek to understand what motivates your teen so you can provide encouragement. Learn to speak your teen's encouragement language. Good advice is not good if your teen does not receive or accept it.

The "E"

The *E* encourages you to exercise sound reasoning in order to develop rational *Expectations* or beliefs. Eliminate irrational expectations and replace them with rational ones.

Occasionally, I interact with parents who fail to properly encourage their teens because they have allowed poor reasoning to evolve into the development of irrational expectations. When teens misbehave, some parents criticize them, cut them off and punish them while expecting and demanding that they respond in a positive manner. Unfortunately, thousands of parents practice this irrational expectation and behavior which is problematic in most parent-teen relationships. Some parents believe that teens cannot learn without being reminded of or punished for their mistakes or shortcomings.

As a society, we have come to believe and expect that change or growth only occurs as a result of punishment and discouragement. I cannot recall the number of times I have observed parents use fear tactics to correct their teens' misbehavior. As I observe such behavior, I ask myself, "How does the parent expect to get positive results from a discouraged and beat-down teen?" Most parents operate under the expectation that punishment and discouragement is the way to correct misbehavior or underachievement. This irrational expectation is one of the major contributors to the development of low self-esteem, insecurity and confusion in teens. Instead of providing proper encouragement when the teen most needs it, some of you contribute to their emotional distress by disrespecting and belittling them.

If you want your teen to do well in life, recognize and praise his efforts instead of placing emphasis on his mistakes. It is vital that you understand that you will get out of your teen what you expect. If your expectations are irrational, your teen will probably respond in an irrational manner. Do not expect your teen to confide in you if you are not willing to listen; do not expect your teen to be open with you if you often tell him that his opinions and comments are stupid or inappropriate. Do not expect to always have logical and smooth conversations with your teen – he does not process like you.

However, do expect that your teen will find someone to confide in and unfortunately, it might be a drug dealer, child predator, womanizer, gang-banger or pimp. To avoid this from occurring, you must eliminate irrational expectations and replace them with positive expectations. Expect the best from your teen and demonstrate respect and trust in his ability. Your teen will succeed if you allow him to engage in personal exploration and provide proper encouragement as he makes decisions. Expect to set the example. The old adage "Do as I say, not as I do" is definitely outdated. Leading by example and providing proper encouragement builds respect and trust in parent-teen relationships.

The "A"

The *A* encourages you to maintain a positive *Attitude* with regard to your teen. Negativity begets negativity. Change starts with you.

Remove negative energy from your household. Any relationship is only as good as the people involved in it. Encouraging parents to understand that they have the ability to set the tempo and standard for their less-experienced teen. In most parent-teen relationships, there will be some level of tension, conflict or disagreement. However, encouraging parents to realize that their attitude will influence how the conflict is resolved. Encouraging parents to strive to maintain a positive attitude about their teens when faced with adversity and conflict.

Developing and maintaining a positive attitude about your teen is one of the most beneficial things that you can do in order to better understand and provide proper encouragement. Recognizing and pointing out positive traits that your teen possesses can help you maintain a positive attitude even during difficult times.

Your attitude about your teen will determine how you interact with him. You should trust and believe that your teen has a positive desire to do right, solve problems and behave in a respectful manner. While this might be difficult to do at times, it must be done because negative views often lead to discouragement and negative responses. If you maintain a positive attitude, provide encouragement, and express respect and trust in your teen, you will have a better chance of decreasing tension between you and him while also eliminating the need to coerce or punish. Respect, faith and trust are attitudes that are synonyms with proper encouragement.

The "L"

The *L* encourages you to develop unconditional *Love* for your teen. Establish a deep, tender, indefinable feeling of affection and attentiveness toward your teen that is not determined or influenced by his behavior.

Do not withdraw your love when your teen disappoints you or does not achieve at the level that you desire. Take pride in being a parent and demonstrate unconditional love. Encouraging parents are proud parents who strive to demonstrate compassion when interacting with their teens. Develop a genuine interest in your teen's life (through good and bad). Demonstrating compassion and unconditional love can lead to honest and sincere interactions. Parents who demonstrate unconditional love strive to bond with their teens out of genuine concern for their personal growth and not out of obligation. Teens are more likely to gravitate toward and connect with parents who are genuine and love them unconditionally. However, you must understand that proper encouragement is a stepping-stone to demonstrating and developing unconditional love in your parent-teen relationship.

The easiest way to show unconditional love for your teen is to praise, accept and love him despite the outcome of his actions. Let your teen know that you will support him regardless of the outcome of his effort. Most parents have difficulty accepting and showing affection to their teens when their behavior is inappropriate or unacceptable. Showing love and affection during difficult times is hard for most parents because many believe that signs of affection might indicate approval of misbehavior or low achievement. This is not accurate because teens need love, affection and encouragement the most when they have failed or misbehaved. God forgives and supports us when we fail or make bad choices and expects us to do the same with our teens. Unconditional love and proper encouragement are closely intertwined because they both remind teens that they will be accepted, loved and appreciated regardless of their behavior or achievements.

The Keep it R.E.A.L. concept provides a road map for providing proper encouragement in your relationship. Learning how to be encouraging is essential to the development of healthy interpersonal skills. The Keep it R.E.A.L. approach is the best method for learning the importance of providing proper encouragement to your teen. It encourages parents to interact with their teens in a respectful, empathic, nonjudgmental and positive manner.

The concept can be essential to saving and restoring troubled relationships, but successful application of the concept requires individuals to be intellectually and emotionally balanced. In order to approach situations realistically and develop rational expectations, you must be capable of thinking clearly and objectively. Additionally, to maintain a positive attitude and develop unconditional love, you must be capable of feeling wholeheartedly and empathically. Providing proper encouragement to your teen is possible if you use the Keep it R.E.A.L. concept, but be aware of old and negative parenting practices that can prevent and limit you from using the concept successfully in your parent-teen relationship.

Parents who seek compliance, strive to correct misbehavior or encourage their teens by using criticism and discouragement are at greater risk for experiencing conflict and tension. Therefore, it important to learn to replace criticizing and discouraging comments with encouraging comments:

Criticizing/Discouraging Comments:

- You never do anything right.
- You always need help.
- You can do better than that.
- You know better so you should not make mistakes.
- Act like you have some common sense.
- You are not creative at all.
- You never try hard enough and always give up.
- Your judgment is poor.
- You never finish anything.

Encouraging Comments:

- You can do anything you put your mind to.
- It is not bad to ask for help as long as you give it your best.
- Your effort was good and things will improve.
- Even the best of us make mistakes.
- I can appreciate what you have to offer.

- Creativity can be developed with effort, time and patience.
- I know you can do it.
- I have confidence in your judgment and know you will figure things out.
- You have made progress and will continue to move forward.

When describing or commenting about teens' behavior you should be mindful that your words can either tear your teen down or build him up. The words listed below highlight the psychological impact of both criticism and proper encouragement.

Criticism	Proper Encouragement
Self-doubt	Confident
Pessimistic	Optimistic
Cold	Empathic
Insecure	Strong sense of self
Confused	In control
Unreliable	Trustworthy
Rebellious	Loyal
Cruel to self	Kind to self
Fear mistakes	Open to mistakes

In summary, teens need proper encouragement just as much as they need love, affection, food, water and shelter. At no other time in our lives do we as human beings struggle with our identity more than we do during our teen years. For that reason, your ability and willingness to provide proper encouragement to your teen should take priority in your relationship. Proper encouragement can equip your teen to approach life realistically, develop rational expectations, maintain a positive attitude and demonstrate unconditional love for himself and others. More importantly, if your teen feels encouraged, he is more likely to demonstrate empathy for others during distressful times.

You must be careful not to allow your position of authority or occasional frustration to negatively influence your ability to properly encourage your teen. Your teen is forming his personality and coping skills daily and he will learn from the adults around him. If you are demanding, insensitive, controlling, belittling and negative, do not get angry with your teen if he displays similar personality traits. As a parent, I encourage you to be proactive about replacing criticism and discouragement with proper encouragement so that your teen can become empowered and feel positive and confident about his abilities and talents. Your ability to create a stimulating, positive and respectful relationship with your teen will come with ease as you learn to focus on your teen's strengths and encourage him more than you criticize him.

TAKE AWAY POINT

Proper encouragement is the key to developing a healthy parent-teen relationship.

QUESTIONS FOR REFLECTION AND PROCESSING

Why is it important to provide proper encouragement?

_____

_____

_____

_____

_____

_____

_____

Can your relationship with your teen blossom if you criticize more than you encourage?

_____

_____

_____

_____

_____

_____

_____

_____

_____

_____

_____

_____

CHAPTER 6

Reinvent Yourself

Become an Empathy-Driven Parent

Y ou are probably asking, "Why do I need to reinvent myself and become an Empathy-Driven Parent? I am glad that you asked. Let me share two very important reasons.

Reason #1: America is experiencing an empathy deficit

America is respected for its democratic way of life meaning every individual has the freedom to think, feel and act as he or she likes. While this is wonderful for all Americans, this country is currently experiencing an empathy deficit. Empathy deficit is defined as a rapid decrease in the expression of compassion and respect for mankind followed by a rapid increase in the expression of unfriendliness, selfishness and self-centeredness.

Over the past two or three decades, the empathy deficit has negatively affected thousands of individuals including parents and teens who have become increasingly insensitive to the emotional needs of one another. Unfortunately, a large percentage of parents and teens are fighting more frequently over issues associated with unresolved anger, bullying, strict household rules, poor academics, sexual orientation, unhappiness and inappropriate peer influence. If you, as a parent, desire to develop a better relationship with your teen and help resolve the empathy deficit in America, becoming an *Empathy-Driven Parent* cannot be optional.

Reason #2: Becoming an Empathy-Driven Parent can increase your *influence* over your teen.

A good number of family therapy experts would agree that parents and family members have the most influence on children during their primary developmental years and play a major role in shaping and influencing children's emotional and intellectual development as they transition into their teen years. Although parents are not "solely" responsible for their teen's development, they play an integral role. Parents who lack empathy generally raise teens who lack empathy.

Our first exposure to interpersonal relationships comes from family interactions. Through direct or indirect observation, we learn certain skills and habits, including how to be empathic from our parents and family members. In therapist sessions, I have learned that teens who grow up in households where empathy is expressed freely and without hesitation are more likely to express empathy freely and without hesitation. The process of learning how to be empathic is strongly influenced by the adults in a teen's life. For example, if your teen witnessed you express remorse, understanding and compassion when interacting with someone in distress, he may have learned that it is appropriate to express empathy when individuals are suffering. On the other hand, if your teen witnessed you express insensitivity and coldness when interacting with someone in distress, he may have learned that it is okay to express coldness when individuals are suffering.

Furthermore, if your teen was abused, observed abuse, received inadequate love or was deprived of compassion and understanding, it is highly likely that he or she will lack empathy for others.

You are primarily held responsible for your teen's behavior and society demands that you teach your teen how to behave like a "civilized" person. Too often, you are reminded of your responsibility to control your teen. This demanding and overwhelming level of responsibility is difficult for most parents and unfortunately has caused many of you to become overly obsessed with controlling your teen.

To avoid being viewed as an inadequate parent with no power, many of you spend a great deal of your time and energy thinking about ways in which you can correct your teen's behavior and maintain control. This controlling and authoritative approach to parenting usually contributes to high levels of tension in parent-teen relationships. Unfortunately, when tension intensifies between you and your teen, your desire to control him or her intensifies as well. Punishment is often used to regain or restore control and to ensure that your teen obeys your instructions. However, what you fail to realize or accept is that no human being, including a teen, can be controlled. Like you, they can simply choose to comply or not with requests or instructions presented to them.

While communicating with parents in psychotherapy and seminars, I remind them that, *"Democracy is a gift from man, but Free Will is a gift from God."* I also remind parents of the importance of demonstrating empathy toward their teens instead of trying to control them. With this in mind, if you do not learn anything else from this book, please understand that human beings were not created to be controlled. Attempts to control others often contributes to increased tension, hatred and/or prolonged conflict. Teens, like other at-risk individuals who feel misunderstood often, engage in rebellious behavior when they perceive or feel that they are treated unjustly or disrespectfully.

Do you realize that your control tactics and lack of empathy toward your teen typically sets the stage for your parent-teen conflict? I ask this question in order to encourage you to reflect. It is not my intent to judge you or imply that you are solely responsible for all conflicts between you and your teen. However, if you do not seek to understand your teen and fail to show empathy, you will likely become frustrated and respond accordingly. This in turn, will cause your teen to respond in a similar manner, thus eliminating or minimizing your ability to understand and resolve any potential underlying emotional distress that your teen might be experiencing.

The most effective method for understanding teens' behavior and minimizing rebellious behavior is to establish empathic relationships where they feel emotionally and physically safe. Empathy is one of the most important interpersonal skills you can give your teen because he or she will learn the importance of open-mindedness, sharing and being generous. However, because empathy develops based on a reciprocal process, you must first establish a respectful and trusting relationship with your teen. Creating such a relationship can be challenging at times, especially when you are frustrated or feel discouraged. Demonstrating empathy toward a teen who is disobedient and repeatedly fails to follow instructions can be tough. Occasionally, you might feel like you are wasting your time; however, you must remember that failure to listen to and demonstrate empathy toward your teen can cause him or her to believe that you do not have their best interest at heart. Translation: *their life is not worth your time.*

Teens who feel that their parents do not care about or understand them are at greater risk for participating in gangs, using drugs, exhibiting violent behavior, and/or connecting with anyone who expresses a genuine concern in their emotional well-being. For example, your distraught daughter might turn to the older boyfriend who comforts her emotionally, but physically abuses her; or your distraught son might confide in troubled peers or gang members who provide acceptance. To prevent such incidences from occurring, I challenge you to learn as much as you can about your teen and his or her development. I also challenge you not to give up on your teen. Remember that you can improve your parenting skills and strengthen your relationship with your teen by equipping yourself with proper knowledge about teen development and behavior.

KNOWLEDGE IS THE EQUALIZER

During your teen's self-discovery years, some of you will experience frustration, anxiety and discouragement, but remember that your teen is depending on you to help him or her make sense out of and cope with the same emotions. On a regular basis, I am asked, "How do I cope with and eliminate negative emotions so I can improve my relationship with my teen?" My reply: "Acquire knowledge about effective parenting and teen-development."

Without knowledge, your relationship with your teen will not blossom. How often do you equip yourself with information that will help you solve or cope with your parent-teen conflict? You can excel in some things in life based on experimentation and practice, however, raising an unpredictable teen is not one of them. I often debate this topic with parents because some of you believe that it is best to learn as you go. Translation: *"On the job training is best. I am learning how to raise my teen. I am practicing becoming a better parent."* This way of thinking is common among parents who believe that the best way to learn something is through experience. They often say, "If you do not have children, how can you understand what it is like to raise one." *I agree partially*.

It is unfortunate that one of the most important aspects of life, developing healthy relationships, is a task that many parents believe can best be accomplished through experimentation and practice. In other areas of life, where we are responsible for others, we are required to study and acquire knowledge before we can perform those tasks. For example, before you can secure your driver's license, you must study the examination book and pass the test. This process was put into place and is enforced to ensure that you do not harm yourself or others when you get on the bi-ways and highways. Why is there no process or plan in place that requires parents to secure knowledge or study before having children?

I deeply believe that individuals have a right to live as they please and to rear children; however, I also believe that children should not be harmed or suffer because their parents are ill-equipped to raise them. Acquiring knowledge about teen development is critical to understanding your teen and having healthy relationships so please do not depend on your experience alone. Vernon Law, a famous baseball player, once stated, "Experience is a hard teacher because she gives the test first and the lesson afterward." Instead of feeling frustrated and discouraged on a daily basis, try equipping yourself with proper knowledge so that you can be adequately prepared for the test – raising an unpredictable teen.

The main difference between psychotherapists and parents is one of knowledge. Psychotherapists are skilled at dealing with teens because we have studied and earned degrees in human behavior and development. In comparison, you love your teen and desire to do right by him, but may lack academic or research-based knowledge about human behavior and development. Can you imagine what your relationship with your teen would be like if you secured proper knowledge and combined it with your love?

If you desire to learn how to be more empathic toward your teen, but are not successful, you should seek counseling, read additional self-help books like this one or attend parenting workshops. Develop a plan for enhancing your knowledge of yourself and your teen. Through education and training, you can be taught to validate your teen's feelings, learn to communicate effectively with him or her and find out how to resolve conflict appropriately. Trying to navigate through your parent-teen relationship without proper knowledge or instructions can lead to disaster. Matthew 15:14 says, "If the blind lead the blind, both shall fall in the ditch." How can you express empathy or teach your teen to be empathic if you do not know how? Empower yourself by acquiring knowledge and applying it. *Remember that acquisition of knowledge is not power; application of knowledge is power.* Lack of understanding and knowledge is the root cause of most parent-teen conflict.

Do not continue to struggle unnecessarily. You should consistently try to learn as much as you can about your teen and develop a better understanding of how to have a healthier relationship with him or her. This means that you should utilize all available resources. Your dedication and commitment to obtaining knowledge will pay off as you become an empathic parent. In the end, your relationship with your teen will flourish and an abundance of happiness and harmony will follow. Becoming an Empathy-Driven Parent will significantly enhance your ability to understand, influence and bond with your teen. Remember that knowledge is the equalizer.

How Does Empathy-Driven Parenting Work

The ability to succeed in the parental role does not occur without some form of training or education. Even the most nurturing, self-driven and well-intended parents require guidance and seek advice from time to time. Based on the fact that parenting is not a natural or common sense skill, but is an essential part of parenthood, it is imperative to learn how to become an empathic parent.

Those who succeed in parenting do not solely rely on their upbringing as the gold template, but equip themselves with knowledge as they endeavor to assist their teens in becoming healthy and productive citizens. It is important to note that *Empathy-Driven Parenting* is one of the most important interpersonal components of building a healthy home environment. It is also important to note that *Empathy-Driven Parenting* is a process-oriented communication skill learned through a combination of training and practice.

Since *Empathy-Driven Parenting* is a process-oriented parenting approach, the primary goal is to identify and discuss emotions that may cause or contribute to your teen's behaviors. Here is a list of positive and negative emotions your teen might experience:

Positive Emotions

Empathy Compassion Confidence Happiness

Pride Joy Excitement Love

Gratitude Honor Satisfaction Respect

Courage Goodness Positivity Relief

Inspired Peaceful Pleasant Capable

Negative Emotions

Anger Fear Disappointment Discomfort
Sadness Embarrassment Disrespect Shame
Lonely Frustrated Irritated Scared
Confused Anxious Annoyed Ignored
Doubtful Depressed Greed Hostility

Familiarizing yourself with these emotions is critical because emotional bonding has a greater impact on humans' ability to love than intellectual bonding. I believe this to be true because *the nurturing process between parents and their children begins and flourishes as a result of emotional bonding, not intellectual bonding.*

The emotions listed above are typically displayed by teens in response to their desires to have their emotional needs met. For most teens, the need to be accepted, approved, important, cared about, trusted, respected, safe, secure, understood, valued, in control, loved, and supported are emotional needs that strongly influence how they will behave. Your primary goal as a parent is to help your teen feel safe enough to discuss his or her emotional needs with you. As you strive to become an empathic parent, you should possess a greater understanding of emotions and apply guidelines from the Five-Step Empathy Model:

1. Apply the Golden Rule
2. Suspend Judgment
3. Focus on Emotional Distress
4. Validate Emotions
5. Resolve Emotional Distress

As you become familiar with and apply the guidelines from my Five-Step Empathy Model, I am confident that you will develop a stronger emotional connection with your teen. You will have an opportunity to practice after you review each step.

Warning! Failure to comply with implementation guidelines as proposed and instructed below can lead to increased frustration and discouragement.

STEP 1: APPLY THE GOLDEN RULE

The first step to becoming an *Empathy-Driven* Parent is to live by the Golden Rule. If you desire to give or receive empathy, it is very important to treat your teen the way you expect to be treated. Do unto your teen as you would have him or her do unto you.

If you struggle to understand your teen, put yourself in his or her shoes and respond to him or her in the same manner in which you would want or expect him or her to respond to you. Identify with your teen's subjective experience by asking yourself, "How would I feel if I were him or her?" Keep in mind that your ability to identify with and comprehend how your teen feels is an important task that must be mastered in order to be successful in empathic parenting.

STEP 2: SUSPEND JUDGMENT

The second step to becoming an *Empathy-Driven Parent* is to suspend judgment. Matthew 7:2-5 reminds us that we will be judged in the same manner in which we judge others. It encourages us not to be hypocrites and to think about our own shortcomings before we preach to others. After reading this, you are probably asking yourself, "Why is suspending judgment important and how it is associated with being an empathic parent?" I am glad you asked.

Suspending judgment is the most important step in the entire process because it empowers you to create an environment built on respect and trust. If your teen feels that you will pass judgment on him, communication will not occur or will end immediately after it begins. Furthermore, suspending judgment is important because it will enable you to engage your teen with an open mind and a clear conscious.

STEP 3: FOCUS ON EMOTIONAL DISTRESS

The third step to becoming an *Empathy-Driven Parent* is to focus on emotional distress and not the cause of it. Completing this step is easy if you comply with step two above. By suspending judgment, you can focus on your teen's emotional distress instead of focusing on why he is in emotional distress. Remember that we all make bad decisions and mistakes occasionally. When your teen is in emotional distress, he or she needs your support and comfort, not a lecture.

STEP 4: VALIDATE EMOTIONS

The fourth step to becoming an *Empathy-Driven Parent* is to validate emotions. What does this mean? It does not mean that you have to agree with how your teen is feeling, but you should acknowledge how he feels. This is challenging for most parents because many of you believe that you are being too lenient or justifying inappropriate behavior if you acknowledge your teen's emotions. This is not the case. Your task in this step is to simply remind your teen that he or she has a right to feel how he or she likes. You should also remind him that you will remove yourself from the situation if he is not willing or capable of discussing his emotions without being disrespectful or aggressive.

STEP 5: RESOLVE EMOTIONAL DISTRESS

The fifth step to becoming an *Empathy-Driven Parent* is to resolve emotional distress before offering solutions. Relieving emotional stress is important because teens, like adults, do not process well when they are very emotional. Moreover, premature problem solving can cause your teen to feel that you are more concerned with "correcting" his behavior than you are with helping him feel better. However, there is one exception to complying with this step: Safety First! Always address safety issues regardless of what your teen thinks or feels.

Dwayne L. Buckingham

EMPATHY-DRIVEN PARENTING EXERCISE

Below is a list of scenarios I have explored with parents in therapy and seminars. Review each scenario and respond as if you were interacting with your teen. Pay close attention to the emotional undertones in each scenario and try to identify the underlying emotions before you respond. After reading each scenario, use the Five-Step Empathy Model as a guide to help you respond. Suggested responses are provided at the end of the chapter.

Scenario #1

Your 15-year-old daughter comes running through the front door after school. She does not speak and before you can say anything, she throws her book bag on the floor and storms into her bedroom. You enter her room. She is lying across her bed and is crying intensely. You ask, "What is wrong?" She replies, "I did not save myself for marriage as you wanted. I had sex with John two weeks ago. I thought he loved me, but he just wanted to have sex. He broke up with me today. I should have listened to you. I knew better."

Underlying emotion (s):

STEP 1: APPLY THE GOLDEN RULE (How would you feel and what would you want?)

_____

_____

_____

_____

_____

_____

STEP 2: SUSPEND JUDGMENT (Keep an open mind)

_____

_____

_____

_____

_____

_____

_____

_____

_____

_____

_____

_____

_____

STEP 3: FOCUS ON EMOTIONAL DISTRESS (What emotion is present and how can you help relieve the distress?)

_____

_____

_____

_____

_____

_____

STEP 4: VALIDATE EMOTIONS (Recognize and express understanding of emotions)

_____

_____

_____

_____

_____

_____

_____

STEP 5: RESOLVE EMOTIONAL DISTRESS (Show compassion and avoid instruction)

_____

_____

_____

_____

_____

_____

_____

PUT IT ALL TOGETHER: (Write your empathy response)

_____

_____

_____

_____

_____

_____

_____

_____

Scenario #2

You receive a phone call from the police department at 8 p.m. in the evening. The officer on the phone tells you that your 14-year-old son was arrested for shoplifting at the mall. You drive to the police department and pick up your son. On the way home, you do not say anything because you are too angry. After arriving home, your son slams the car door behind him and storms in the house.

You approach him and say, "I do not know what is wrong with you, but you better explain yourself before I beat it out of you." Your son replies, "You never ask me if anything is wrong unless I am in trouble. I only get attention when I am mad. I attempted to steal the shirt because the other boys told me that I had to do something bad to be friends with them."

Underlying emotion (s):

STEP 1: APPLY THE GOLDEN RULE (How would you feel and what would you want?)

_____

_____

_____

_____

_____

_____

_____

STEP 2: SUSPEND JUDGMENT (Keep an open-mind)

_____

_____

_____

_____

_____

_____

STEP 3: FOCUS ON EMOTIONAL DISTRESS (What emotion is present and how can you help relieve the distress?)

_____

_____

_____

_____

_____

_____

_____

STEP 4: VALIDATE EMOTIONS (Recognize and express understanding of emotions)

_____

_____

_____

_____

_____

_____

_____

STEP 5: RESOLVE EMOTIONAL DISTRESS
(Show compassionate and avoid instruction)

_____

_____

_____

_____

_____

_____

PUT IT ALL TOGETHER: (Write your empathy

response)

_____

_____

_____

_____

_____

_____

_____

_____

_____

_____

_____

Scenario #3

You receive your telephone bill and see $200 worth of calls to a sex hotline. You approach your 12-year-old son and ask, "Did you call a sex hotline?" He replies, "I did not call any sex hotlines. You always accuse me of something." You respond, "You better tell me the truth." He says, "I do not feel comfortable talking to you about sex. My friend told me to check it out because I asked him some questions. Everybody is talking about the hotline at school and I did not want to be left out. I knew you would be upset."

Underlying emotion (s):

STEP 1: APPLY THE GOLDEN RULE (How would you feel and what would you want?)

_____

_____

_____

_____

_____

_____

_____

STEP 2: SUSPEND JUDGMENT (Keep an open mind)

_____

_____

_____

_____

_____

_____

_____

STEP 3: FOCUS ON EMOTIONAL DISTRESS (What emotion is present and how can you help relieve the distress?)

_____

_____

_____

_____

_____

_____

_____

STEP 4: VALIDATE EMOTIONS (Recognize and express understanding of emotions)

_____

_____

_____

_____

_____

_____

_____

STEP 5: RESOLVE EMOTIONAL DISTRESS (Show compassion and avoid instruction)

_____

_____

_____

_____

_____

_____

PUT IT ALL TOGETHER: (Write your empathy response)

_____

_____

_____

_____

_____

_____

_____

Scenario #4

Your 17-year-old daughter approaches you and asks if she can go to the mall with her friend. You say yes. She leaves your home with a bag in her hand and heads down the street to her friend's house. Ten minutes later, you receive a phone call from one of your female neighbors. She tells you that she saw your daughter walking down the street wearing a very short dress with most of her backside showing.

Your daughter returns home two hours later, but is not wearing the short dress. You ask, "Did you change clothes after you left home." She replies, "Yes, I put on a different dress." You ask, "Was it appropriate? Did you look presentable?" Your daughter replies, "Yes, it was presentable. All the girls are wearing the same thing." You reply, "I was told that your backside was hanging out." Your daughter says, "Are you spying on me. That is not fair. I just want to fit in and look fashionable like everybody else."

Underlying emotion (s):

STEP 1: APPLY THE GOLDEN RULE (How would you feel and what would you want?)

_____

_____

_____

_____

_____

_____

_____

STEP 2: SUSPEND JUDGMENT (Keep an open mind)

_____

_____

_____

_____

_____

STEP 3: FOCUS ON EMOTIONAL DISTRESS (What emotion is present and how can you help relieve the distress?)

_____

_____

_____

_____

_____

_____

STEP 4: VALIDATE EMOTIONS (Recognize and express understanding of emotions)

_____

_____

_____

_____

_____

_____

STEP 5: RESOLVE EMOTIONAL DISTRESS (Show compassion and avoid instruction)

_____

_____

_____

_____

_____

_____

PUT IT ALL TOGETHER: (Write your empathy response)

_____

_____

_____

_____

_____

_____

_____

Scenario #5

Your 13-year-old son approaches you and asks if he can have a Facebook page because he wants to communicate with his friends. You say, "You are not old enough to be on Facebook or any other social media network." Your son replies, "You act like I am a baby. I do what I am supposed to do when told so I don't know why you always try to limit what I do."

Underlying emotion (s):

STEP 1: APPLY THE GOLDEN RULE (How would you feel and what would you want?)

_____

_____

_____

_____

_____

_____

STEP 2: SUSPEND JUDGMENT (Keep an open mind)

_____

_____

_____

_____

STEP 3: FOCUS ON EMOTIONAL DISTRESS (What emotion is present and how can you help relieve the distress?)

_____

_____

_____

_____

_____

_____

STEP 4: VALIDATE EMOTIONS (Recognize and express understanding of emotions)

_____

_____

_____

_____

_____

_____

STEP 5: RESOLVE EMOTIONAL DISTRESS (Show compassion and avoid instruction)

_____

_____

_____

_____

_____

_____

_____

_____

PUT IT ALL TOGETHER: (Write your empathy response)

_____

_____

_____

_____

_____

_____

Scenario #6

Your 16-year-old son approaches you and tells you that he is addicted to drugs. He says, "I started using drugs while hanging out with friends at school. We used marijuana initially and started experimenting with other drugs. I have been stealing things from home and selling them to support my addiction. I apologize for stealing from you and ruining my life."

Underlying emotion (s):

STEP 1: APPLY THE GOLDEN RULE (How would you feel and what would you want?)

_____

_____

_____

_____

_____

_____

_____

STEP 2: SUSPEND JUDMENT (Keep an open mind)

_____

_____

_____

_____

_____

_____

_____

STEP 3: FOCUS ON EMOTIONAL DISTRESS (What emotion is present and how can you help relieve the distress?)

_____

_____

_____

_____

_____

STEP 4: VALIDATE EMOTIONS (Recognize and express understanding of emotions)

_____

_____

_____

_____

_____

STEP 5: RESOLVE EMOTIONAL DISTRESS (Show compassion and avoid instruction)

_____

_____

_____

_____

_____

_____

_____

PUT IT ALL TOGETHER: (Write your empathy response)

_____

_____

_____

_____

_____

_____

_____

_____

_____

_____

_____

_____

_____

Conclusion

Although *Empathy-Driven Parenting* should occur before your child reaches his or her teen years, learning to be empathic is a skill that teens must also learn and master in order to thrive emotionally and intellectually. Human development is a continuous process, which means that you and I, like your teen, are growing and changing every day of our lives. Unfortunately, some of you have given up on your teen because you are convinced that he or she is set in his or her ways and cannot be reached. You may also be convinced that processing emotions will not help your situation because it does not offer any solutions.

I understand that you may be concerned about the effectiveness of processing emotions with your teen. You may be more comfortable with implementing behavioral interventions and discipline, but I advise you not to minimize the power of understanding and processing emotions with your teen. Contrary to popular belief, you cannot truly address or resolve any conflict or distress without understanding its root cause. No matter how frustrated or discouraged you may have felt in the past, you now understand what it takes to become an Empathy-Driven Parent.

As a parent, you are totally capable of understanding and influencing your teen by becoming an Empathy-Driven Parent and gifting them the gift of empathy. The compassion that you show your teen will extend into his or her life and beyond. Empathy-Driven Parenting is not guaranteed to resolve all of the problems that arise between you and your teen, but it will set the stage for a loving, caring and compassionate relationship. After all, your teen will one day become an adult and possibly a parent. Given this, you can find comfort in knowing that your gift of empathy will have an impact on generations to come.

Resources

You may find the following resources helpful if you want to further explore areas of interest or concern. The list is by no means exhaustive; nor can I endorse every point in every book. But you will find plently of valuable information that will supplement what you read in this book.

OTHER EMPATHY FOCUSED BOOKS

Borba, M. *UnSelfie: Why Empathetic Kids Succeed in Our All-About-Me World* (2017).

Elliot, A. *Why Can't My Child Behave?: Empathic Parenting Strategies That Work for Adoptive and Foster Families* (2013)

Bruce D. Perry, Maia Szalavitz, et al. *Born for Love: Why Empathy Is Essential – and Endangered.* (2015)

Faber, A. & Mazlish, E. *How to Talk So Teens Will Listen and Listen So Teens Will Talk* (2005)

Goleman, Daniel. *Emotional Intelligence: Why It Can Matter More Than IQ.* (2005).

Gottman, John. *The Heart of Parenting: Raising an Emotionally Intelligent Child* (1998).

Dyer, Judy. *Empath: A Complete Guide for Developing Your Gift and Finding Yourself.* (2017).

Scheduling for Seminars or Speaking Engagements

Broadening Horizons by Facilitating *R.E.A.L.* Change

Dr. Buckingham conducts educational wellness seminars for individuals, families, groups, churches and organizations throughout the year.

"Gifting Empathy" is one of the most requested seminars; however, Dr. Buckingham conducts seminars on a variety of topics.

To book a training or conference:

R.E.A.L. Horizons Consulting Solutions, LLC
8101 Sandy Spring, Rd Suite. 250
Laurel, MD 20707

240-240-1008 Voice Mail
www.realhorizonsdlb.com

I hope this book has been a blessing to you and

I welcome your comments.
dwayne@realhorizonsdlb.com

This book can also be purchased online at:

www.realhorizonsdlb.com

Amazon.com

About the Author

DWAYNE L BUCKINGHAM, PH.D., LCSW-C, BCD is President & CEO of R.E.A.L. Horizons Consulting Solutions, LLC. As a decorated veteran and renowned empathy and resilience expert he has provided psychological assessments, treatment and psycho-educational training to over 30,000 individuals, couples, groups, and families worldwide.

Dr. Buckingham is driven by the belief that every individual can improve his or her ability to cope with life challenges productively if given the opportunity and right support. He reminds individuals daily that a little understanding and education eliminates barriers and enables individuals to grow. Dr. Buckingham appears in the media on a regular basis and views his role as community consultant. Through consultation and training, he hopes to provide individuals with the knowledge and skills essential to establishing and maintaining a positive and productive lifestyle.

Whether working with organizations as a consultant, providing counseling services or coaching leaders, Dr. Buckingham supports parents who are committed to raising empathetic children.

To learn more about Dr. Buckingham, please visit his website at www.realhorizonsdlb.com for more information.